# The Best Pet Tales Ever

## Starring Sweetie Pie and Sam

Written by
**Stan and Carol Hall**

Illustrated by
**Marvin Paracuelles**

Order this book online at www.trafford.com
or email orders@trafford.com

Most Trafford titles are also available at major online book retailers.

© Copyright 2013 Stan and Carol Hall.

All rights reserved. No part of this publication may be reproduced, stored in a retrieval system, or transmitted, in any form or by any means, electronic, mechanical, photocopying, recording, or otherwise, without the written prior permission of the author.

Printed in the United States of America.

ISBN: 978-1-4907-0610-8 (sc)
       978-1-4907-0609-2 (e)

Library of Congress Control Number: 2013914369

Because of the dynamic nature of the Internet, any web addresses or links contained in this book may have changed since publication and may no longer be valid. The views expressed in this work are solely those of the author and do not necessarily reflect the views of the publisher, and the publisher hereby disclaims any responsibility for them.

Our mission is to efficiently provide the world's finest, most comprehensive book publishing service, enabling every author to experience success. To find out how to publish your book, your way, and have it available worldwide, visit us online at www.trafford.com

Any people depicted in stock imagery provided by Thinkstock are models,
and such images are being used for illustrative purposes only.
Certain stock imagery © Thinkstock.

Trafford rev. 08/30/2013

 www.trafford.com

North America & international
toll-free: 1 888 232 4444 (USA & Canada)
fax: 812 355 4082

## Table of Contents

The Chase .................................................................. 2

Trash Talk ................................................................. 6

The Trip.................................................................... 10

Checkup Day ........................................................... 16

Guarding the Yard ..................................................... 22

The Beach ............................................................... 28

I'd like to tell a story
To someone just like you.

Everything that happened is absolutely true
And if you don't believe me
You can ask my sister, Sue.

There is a kitty named Sweetie Pie
And a little dog named Sam.
My sister likes Sweetie Pie
But she is not too fond of Sam.

Sam likes to chase the kitty
My sister likes to hold
And Sweetie Pie gets nervous
When Sam starts getting bold.

Her legs get stiff, her tail goes up
And her little back gets arched
Her claws come out, her teeth are bared
She hates Sam's awful bark.

My sister started screaming
Because the kitty's on her knee.

And then I started laughing
Because it's fun to see
And because I'm really glad
The kitty's not on me.

My sister was excited
And she tried to stop the squall
And then the kitty jumped from her
And hung right from the wall.

Sam was really happy
He wanted the kitty to jump some more
And the kitty's legs were running
When she fell back to the floor.

Sam likes to chase the kitty
So he knew just what to do
And it's a good thing he started running
Because he's got to get away from Sue.

So Sweetie Pie is running
And Sam is running too
And behind the both of them
Is coming Sister Sue.

The kitty needs a place to hide
And sees a big trash can
So in she jumps and thinks she's safe
But watch out, here comes Sam.

He wants to catch that kitty
And get away from Sue
So I'll bet you'll never guess
What he decides to do.

Well, things were happening really fast
He wasn't thinking right
And Sam just likes to chase, you know
He doesn't like to fight.

Now when you jump into a can
There isn't any space
And Sweetie Pie and Sam were there
Standing face to face.

Now Sam just thought that he had won
He thought the chase was through
But really, he was trapped, you know
Between Sweetie Pie and Sue.

The kitty bites and scratches
Sue gives Sam a cuff
This isn't good for Sammy—now
I think he's had enough.

He's had to get away from there
He doesn't like to fight.
It was just a little chase, you know
This fighting can't be right.

Sammy yelps and whimpers
He goes *Aroo! Aroo!*
He's running for his own bed now
It's the safest thing to do.

He has to escape from Sweetie Pie
And get away from Sue.

He makes it to his pillow
And they have stayed behind
He licks his little scratches
They'll be better in no time.

He's going to have a little rest
He'll wake up good as new
And then he'll go looking
For Sweetie Pie and Sue.

And if they have another adventure
I can maybe tell it to you too.

I'd like to tell a story
To someone just like you.

And everything that happened
Is absolutely true
And if you don't believe me
You can ask my sister Sue.

There is a kitty named Sweetie Pie
And a little dog named Sam
My sister likes the Sweetie Pie
But she's not too fond of Sam.

We had enjoyed a holiday dinner
And it had been quite a day
But the house was back in order
And the leftovers were put away.

The bones and extra trimmings
Had been put into the trash
There were packages and soggy bits
It had really been a bash.

The can was a bit too full of stuff
The lid wasn't on quite tight
But it was going out tomorrow
So it should have been all right.

The TV was playing
The show was kind of good
And Sweetie Pie was on the couch
Being where she should.

But Sam was in the kitchen
That can was on his mind
It was the bestest treasure
A little dog could find.

All those bits and pieces
He just had to have a look
He knew they would never miss
The little things he took.

He was pulling out the pieces
He spread them on the floor
Every piece was just so good
He had to get some more.

He had been there awhile
He was getting kind of full
*Just one more piece* is what he thought
So he grabbed and gave a pull.

Over came the whole darn can
Lid and trash and all
Sister Sue came running
To see what had made the fall.

The kitchen floor was just a mess
The can was on its side
Sam was just standing there
There was no place to hide.

Sue made such an awful scream
When she rushed into the room
All that she could think to do
Was whack him with the broom.

Well, Sammy had been snacking
A bit more than he should
And Sister Sue didn't know it yet
But he didn't feel too good.

So she whacked him with the broom
And gave him a little kick
Sammy was too full to run
But he got a little sick.

Oh, you should have heard the sound she made
You should have seen her look
You should have seen her stomping feet
As she gagged and choked and shook.

That was it for Sammy
It was an awful plight
She tied a leash around his neck
He was staying out tonight.

Sammy didn't like being out
Unless it was to prowl
And since he didn't feel too good
He decided he would howl.

I had to help clean up the trash
'Cause Sue was going to cry
And even though I'd have liked her help
There was no way she'd try.

But she was quite eager
To let us all know
Of some of the awful, horrible places
She thought Sam should go.

So Sam was on the porch
There was nothing we could do
We just had to let him howl
*Arooo! Arooo! Arooo!*

He'll soon start feeling better
It was just the trash-can flu
And tomorrow when he wakes up
He'll be feeling good as new.

And then he'll go looking
For Sweetie Pie and Sue
And if they have another adventure
I can maybe tell it to you too.

I'd like to tell a story
To someone just like you.

And everything that happened
Is absolutely true
And if you don't believe me
You can ask my sister Sue.

There is a kitty named Sweetie Pie
And a little dog named Sam
My sister likes the Sweetie Pie
But she's not too fond of Sam.

We were going to the beach
We were going there today
We were going to see the wind and waves
We were going there to play.

It was a little ways to go
We were going in the car
We were taking Sweetie Pie and Sam
It really wasn't far.

We put the kitty in a box
Sue held it on her knee
Sam was sitting in the back
He was riding there with me.

Sweetie Pie liked riding
If we aren't going far
But she was a little nervous
'Cause Sam was in the car.

I had the window open
So my face could feel wind blow
Sammy likes to do that too
And likes to watch where we might go.

He had crawled up on top of me
And had his head stuck out
His ears were flopping in the breeze
The wind swelled up his snout.

His eyes were closed like little slits
It was hard for him to see
And his mouth was hanging open
When he was hit by that big bee.

Mr. Bee wasn't happy
When he bumped into Sammy's tongue
So he got his stinger out
And he stuck it in and stung.

Sammy's tongue was burning
You know what hot is like for you
He never saw the bee, you know
He just yelped *Arooo! Arooo!*

He knew his tongue was really hurt
He wasn't sure just why
It felt the very same to him
As getting clawed by Sweetie Pie.

Sam decided it must be the kitty
Who was causing his new grief
Even though it was not true
This was truly his belief.

Now Sweetie Pie was riding
In an open box with Sue
And they were not prepared at all
With what Sam decided he should do.

It wasn't one of his better plans
It might be better classed as bad
But he made it really quick, you know
When he was hurt and getting mad.

He came back in the window
And gave Sweetie Pie a nip
He never even thought about us
Being on a trip.

The chase was on inside the car
The kitty wanted out
Sam jumped in the front with Sue
You should have heard her shout.

The kitty bounced off my mom
Off the seat and Sue and me
The driving was erratic
Mom was heading for a tree.

We were all screaming
We thought our lives were over
My momma gave the car a swerve
And skidded through a field of clover.

Sometimes bad things happen
But everything's still OK
My mom said we wouldn't push our luck
We were calling it a day.

We took a little minute
We took a small time-out
We needed time to wonder
What that had been about.

It wasn't a normal act, you know
For Sam to give the cat a bite
Sam likes to do a lot of things
But he doesn't like to fight.

I told my mom each detail
That I could think to tell
She figured out the rest
When Sam's tongue began to swell.

But she said it never mattered
What I thought that Sam had thunk
She was taking us back home now
And he was riding in the trunk.

Sue calmed down the Sweetie Pie
And got her ready for the ride
She put the kitty in the box
Then made sure the box was tied.

As soon as we got home
We opened the trunk door
Sammy was curled up in there
And his tongue was getting sore.

He didn't seem that anxious
To give up his new nest
So we got him cool water
And let him have a rest.

And later when he wakes up
He'll be good as new
Then he'll go looking
For Sweetie Pie and Sue.

And if he has another adventure
I could maybe tell it to you too.

I'd like to tell a story
To someone just like you.

And everything that happened
Is absolutely true
And if you don't believe me
You can ask my sister Sue.

There is a kitty named Sweetie Pie
And a little dog named Sam
My sister liked the Sweetie Pie
But she's not too fond of Sam.

It was that awful time again
The time both Sam and the kitty fear
It was time to see the vet again
Yes, it was that time of year.

A trip to see the doctor!
If they knew, they'd make a fuss
Sometimes we have adventures
That are not good fun for us.

He'd probably check them over
He'd poke and prod and pick
He'd look at their teeth and tongue and ears
And make sure they were not sick.

He would see if they were too heavy
He would know if they were not
He would check their fur and feet and tail
He'd give them both a shot.

We knew to keep it secret
We knew not to let them know
We knew they did not like it there
We knew they would not want to go.

We packed their favorite toys and treats
The ones we play with at the park
Sam got all excited
He began to bark.

They were getting really eager
To go out and play
We had them fooled about the vet
Which was our plan today.

Sam knew something wasn't right
We weren't at his favorite place
And when he realized where we were
You should have seen his face.

He wasn't happy anymore
The kitty knew it too
And when we got right to the door
They were not going through.

Sam was stiff and shaking
He had a scared look in his eye
Sister Sue had used her coat
And wrapped up Sweetie Pie.

The doctor vet came over
He said, "And how are you?"
Sammy was still shaking
And he piddled on his shoe.

We had to get some paper
And clean his floor and shoe
Sue was so embarrassed
But sometimes that's what doggies do.

Sue said she would wait outside
When we were done to " give her a call"
She handed him the Sweetie Pie
She gave him coat and all.

The kitty gave a warning hiss
He should have never made that pause
She scrambled free from the coat
She was all teeth and claws.

He had to get her off of him
He was getting scratched real bad
You should never hold an upset kitty
Especially if she's mad.

All of this excitement was making
Sam's mind race
If he could chase a kitty
This wouldn't be such an awful place.

The doctor held the kitty
Gently by the throat
And with a twisty pull
He got her off his coat.

Kitty was so happy
To be free upon the floor
And in a flash both she and Sam
Were through the office door.

Sam was feeling better
He barked when Sweetie Pie was freed
He had her hanging from the drapes
He had the kitty treed.

He was very proud
As he watched the kitty swing
So the doctor put him on the table
And did his checkup thing.

And when he got his needle
He didn't even feel it sting.

Then we called for Sister Sue
She was outside, not far
And gave her Sam to take away
And put him in the car.

We had to catch the Sweetie Pie
For her visit with the vet
We wrapped her in the coat again
He didn't really trust her yet.

He did his poke and prodding
He did a thorough check
And since we had her tightly wrapped
She got the needle in her neck.

Sam and the kitty are healthy
They'll probably stay that way
We won't do this for another year
So all in all it went OK.

Sometimes the little needles
Make them sleep an hour or two
We'll get them home and rested
And they'll wake up good as new.

And once again Sam will go looking
For Sweetie Pie and Sue
And if they have another adventure
I can maybe tell it to you too.

I'd like to tell a story
To someone just like you.

And everything that happened
Is absolutely true
And if you don't believe me
You can ask my sister Sue.

There is a kitty named Sweetie Pie
And a little dog named Sam
My sister likes the Sweetie Pie
But she's not too fond of Sam.

Sam was lying on the steps
And knew he was the king
Of everything that he could see
He was the king of everything.

Sweetie Pie was sunning
She didn't feel like playing hard
But she really enjoyed lying on the grass
In our backyard.

The neighbor's dog was going by
He was on the prowl
When Sammy saw him going by
He gave a warning growl.

The neighbor doggy heard him
But he didn't pay any heed
And he no sooner spotted Sweetie Pie
And he had that kitty treed.

At least for Sweetie Pie
A tree had been her goal
But she had made a small mistake
And climbed the hydro pole.

Hydro poles are really high
And there is no place to stop
So if you're going to sit on one
You must get right to the top.

Sam could not believe it
His hackles gave a throb
If someone's chasing kitties
King Sam would do the job.

That awful dog was barking
And chasing the kitty up the pole
So Sammy jumped on top of him
And they began to roll.

It was a fearsome tussle
That other dog was tough
Now Sam didn't like fighting
But he too was tough enough.

When other dogs come in your yard
The yard in which you are king
You simply must protect it
You got to do your thing.

Sometimes when dogs are fighting
They get really loud
People began to gather
They formed a little crowd.

Everyone was watching
And wanted them apart
But touching fighting dogs
You know, isn't very smart.

Sister Sue came running
With the garden hose turned on
She hosed them with cold water
Right there on the lawn.

The prowling dog could not win
It had to be that way
This was Sammy's only yard
The other dog couldn't stay.

Sue was busy squirting
Both the dogs all right
She was teaching them a lesson
She was teaching them not to fight.

The other dog knew he had to go
Now that he was wet and bit and sore
He broke free and started running
I bet he won't come back no more.

The excitement now was over
And that was the end of that
Now we had to figure out
How to save the cat.

Sue was not happy
Because her Sweetie Pie was stuck
She had to get her rescued
So she called the hydro truck.

Kitty was getting worried
That pole was much too high
She could not just jump down
But she looked like she would try.

Sam liked all the action
He tried to climb the pole
But he couldn't get any traction
So he thought he'd dig a hole.

He was running round in circles
His antics finally got her
He over did it with his barking
So Sue sprayed him with more water.

Soon the bucket truck arrived
They were good at what they do
In absolutely no time
They did a Sweetie Pie rescue.

Sue was getting calm now
She put the hose away
She took the kitty in the house
Where it was safe to stay.

The crowd had started leaving
And were discussing everything
Sam went back up on the steps
And continued being king.

He was still a little wet
And he had a bruise or two
He'll probably have a little rest
And wake up good as new.

And then he'll go looking
For Sweetie Pie and Sue
And if he has another adventure
Then maybe I can tell it to you too.

I'd like to tell a story
To someone just like you.

Everything that happened is absolutely true
And if you don't believe me
You can ask my sister Sue.

There is a kitty named Sweetie Pie
And a little dog named Sam
My sister likes the Sweetie Pie
But she is not too fond of Sam.

It was the summertime
A warm and sunny day
We had travelled to the beach
It was time to go and play.

We had a lot to do
To get it set up right
We planned to stay all day
And maybe half the night.

We had some stuff to carry
And we all followed Sue
She'd been here before
And knew exactly what to do.

Sweetie Pie and she
Were going to have some fun
With a blanket on the beach
And lying in the sun.

We had a cooler and some groceries
We had a chopping maul
We made Sue a little shelter
We built her up a wall.

We circled stones to make a fire
We collected extra wood
If the weather became cooler
A fire would be good.

I had a pail and shovel
So we could gather
Clams and shells
Sam wanted to explore the beach
And check out all the smells.

The ocean tide was running
It was going out
"You and Sam be careful!"
I heard my sister shout.

There were rocks and sand and water
Flocks of birds were everywhere
Buried clams were squirting
Streams of water in the air.

The tidal pools are super great
With fifty colors—maybe more
Crabs and starfish on the walls
Fish flashing near the floor.

There were barnacles and limpets
Mussels, worms, and slugs
Shrimps and crawly creatures
And a hundred kinds of bugs.

The anemones and seaweed
Looked like little flowers
Time goes so fast at the beach
With things to do for hours.

If Sam was running through the water
And a flock of birds skimmed by
He'd jump and splash toward them
Then off the flock would fly.

Then he discovered something
Moving underneath a rock
So he stuck his nose in
But got an awful shock.

A set of crabby pinchers
Caught him by the snout
And pinched his nose
So hard and tight
His head could not come out.

He pulled until it hurt
It scared him, I think too
I rushed to try and help him
As he yelped *Aroo! Aroo!*

He pulled again, but harder
This time he got it free
So I checked his nose out
To see what I could see.

He had a little cut
And the starting of a swell
But that wasn't stopping Sammy
With still so many things to smell.

Off he went exploring
Then discovered his best wish
He found a stinky pile
Of horrid-smelling fish.

He rolled and rolled all over it
And got it in his hair
'Till he had clumps of stinky fish
On him everywhere.

He thought he smelled really good
He thought she would like it too
So off he went running
To show himself to Sue.

He got beside her blanket
And shook off the wet and sand
She shouted, "Sammy, quit that!"
And pushed him with her hand.

She felt the slimy goo
Matted in his fur
She rubbed her fingers on her shirt
And got the smell on her.

Then she finally noticed
The awful, horrid smell
"Oh, you rotten stinky dog!"
I could hear her yell.

Sammy was in trouble
It was time for him to run
He was very, very lucky
Sue never had a gun.

And just like that she packed our cooler
And our day was done
She was mad at me and Sam
'Cause we had ruined the fun.

Everything was gathered
Off we went for home
So she could scrub poor Sammy
With a mop and soapy foam.

She was going to clean him
Till he was cleaner than her cat
She was going to teach him
It was bad to smell like that.

Now Sammy hated being bathed
And it took more than an hour
Even worse, she perfumed him
With "special lilac flower."

Finally, she has him finished
And it's time for her own shower
I'll bet you anything you want
She'll be gone another hour.

Now Sammy smells like perfume
And his nose is getting sore
So he curls up in his bed
And soon begins to snore.

He dreams of being at the beach
He dreams of birds and fish
He dreams of chasing kitties
And his favorite doggy dish.

He dreams of running at the park
He dreams of me and Sue
He dreams of all his favorite things
That he just loves to do.

He's going to have his little rest
He'll wake up good as new
And then he'll go looking
For Sweetie Pie and Sue.

And if they have another adventure
I can maybe tell it to you too.